The Well-Seasoned Skillet

Emma,
Hope you enjoy!
Best Wishes,
Kim McCallie
2017

D1456726

The Well-Seasoned Skillet

68 of the Best One-Pan Recipes

Kimberly McCallie

author of *Southern on a Shoestring*

FRONT TABLE BOOKS | AN IMPRINT OF CEDAR FORT, INC. | SPRINGVILLE, UTAH

ISBN 13: 978-1-4621-1981-3
Published by Front Table Books, an imprint of Cedar Fort, Inc.
2373 W. 700 S., Springville, UT 84663
Distributed by Cedar Fort, Inc., www.cedarfort.com

LIBRARY OF CONGRESS CATALOGING-IN-PUBLICATION DATA

Names: McCallie, Kimberly, 1969- author.
Title: The well-seasoned skillet / Kimberly McCallie.
Description: Springville, Utah : Front Table Books, an imprint of Cedar Fort,
  Inc., [2017] | Includes index.
Identifiers: LCCN 2016053066 (print) | LCCN 2016055155 (ebook) | ISBN
  9781462119813 (perfect bound : alk. paper) | ISBN 9781462127504 (epub,
  pdf, mobi)
Subjects: LCSH: Skillet cooking. | LCGFT: Cookbooks.
Classification: LCC TX840.S55 M33 2017 (print) | LCC TX840.S55 (ebook) | DDC
  641.7/7--dc23
LC record available at https://lccn.loc.gov/2016053066

Cover and page design by M. Shaun McMurdie
Cover design © 2017 by Cedar Fort, Inc.
Edited by Jennifer Johnson

Printed in the United States of America

10 9 8 7 6 5 4 3 2 1

Printed on acid-free paper

To my mama, Susan Fort,
who was brave enough to make a better life for us.

Contents

Breakfast & Appetizers

Side Dishes

Main Dishes

Acknowledgments

To Judith Shuman who continues to support and encourage me through this harrowing journey of life. It means everything to still have you in my corner.

To Kristie Long and Melodie Fulcher, who bring friendship, laughter, and unwavering support into my life. I miss you both on a daily basis.

To my Mema, Ada Toole, who will never know how far-reaching her influence has been on all of us. Some of the best memories of my life took place in your kitchen.

To the memory of three special ladies, Cynthia, Fonnie, and Alice. I remember you all with love and miss your existence in my life.

To my husband, Eric, who still believes that something good will come from being married to me.

Everybody Has a Story

Everybody has a story; some people tell it better than others. If you have a little time, sit down and I'll tell you mine.

My great-granddaddy was the cook in the family. He was also a kind and gentle man who would load me into my little red wagon and pull me to a nearby general store to purchase a bag of penny candy. He died when I was six, so my memories of him are limited, but when I do think of him, I remember him standing in front of the stove. My mama remembers him as an attentive cook who nursed his food along and never left its side until it was ready to be served. I have inherited that gene.

While many people love the idea of throwing a bunch of ingredients into a slow cooker and leaving it unattended for hours while it simmers away, I do not share that passion for convenience. Preparing a meal in a slow cooker does not allow me to actually cook. The acts of searing, turning, stirring, seasoning, and testing are why I find so much satisfaction in cooking. Yes, the end means of cooking is to put a meal on the table, but I also must enjoy the process along the way.

Until recently, I cooked on a one-burner stove. It wasn't made that way. It started out as a regular four-burner stove, but over the years, the burners went out one by one. Being an adaptive creature, I just adjusted my cooking style along the way. When I was down to one burner, I learned very quickly that I needed to stick with meals that I could cook in one pot or skillet. Cooking in a skillet proved to be a quicker process, so it became my preferred method of cooking.

I found that I could cook anything in a skillet. I could boil pasta in a skillet. After the pasta was cooked, I would use a colander scoop or a pasta spoon to transfer the pasta to a bowl. I would allow the pasta water to cool until it was safe to move the skillet, and then I would pour out the remaining pasta water, wipe out the skillet, and begin the rest of the dish. I also cooked rice in a skillet. While some of my skillets had lids to cover the rice, I also made "lids" from metal pie plates, round cake pans, and aluminum foil. I just kept pot holders and oven mitts at the ready so I wouldn't burn myself. I may as well have been cooking on a chuck wagon during the western expansion.

My History with Skillets

I've never been able to build a lasting relationship with cast-iron skillets. My mom has an iron griddle, black and smooth with years of use making pancakes and grilled cheeses. When I met my husband, he had a small cast-iron skillet that he used regularly—the operative word there being *had*. Then I came along into his life and things changed, not all for the better.

One weekend while we were dating, his parents came to visit and his dad used the skillet to fry an egg for breakfast that morning. I arrived at Eric's apartment right after breakfast, and, calling myself helping, I removed the skillet from the stove and placed it on a pot holder. Now, apparently, these black iron skillets get hot—really hot—so hot that it burned and melted the pot holder to the bottom of the skillet. Oops!

About this time, Eric walked through the kitchen and saw the mess. Feeling guilty, I didn't make eye contact or even mention what had happened. He assessed the damage and said, "I can't believe Dad did that!" Before I could clarify, he walked away, and I tried to salvage the skillet by placing it in a sink full of hot, soapy water—pot holder and all. Then his dad walked through the kitchen and saw the soaking skillet, then said, "I can't believe Eric did that!"

I was too far in by this point, so I quickly removed the skillet (pot holder and all) from the sink, dried it off as well as I could, and hid it in a cabinet. I intended to fix things later, but ended up throwing the whole thing away with the pot holder still stuck to the bottom.

Shameful, I know! It wasn't one of my finest moments and I'm not proud of it. Amused by it? Yes! But not proud.

My friend Deborah encouraged me to purchase and season cast iron skillets using the following method: "Take some grease (shortening) and grease that baby real good (all over) inside and out. Put it in the oven and bake it, bake it, bake it! On 350 or 400 degrees. It will take several times doing this. I wouldn't wash it until I had it seasoned. Just add some more grease and keep baking."

About This Cookbook

Currently, I use both cast-iron and nonstick skillets. The skillet sizes I used in these recipes are between 9½" and 12", so if you have skillets within that range, you should be set. These recipes are designed with no specific type of skillet in mind. If you currently have a skillet, cast-iron or nonstick, that you are comfortable using and have had great success with in the kitchen, please use it.

Tips:

- *All of my rice dishes were cooked in a 9½" nonstick skillet. If you cook rice in a larger skillet, you may need to reduce the cooking time since the skillet will have more surface area. I suggest checking the rice at the 15-minute mark.*

- *Several of the recipes in this cookbook require the skillet to be covered during the cooking process. If you don't have a lid, you may want to consider purchasing a universal lid or silicon lid if you're planning to cook those dishes. They're fairly inexpensive and are readily available in most stores.*

- *Several of the recipes list prepared pasta as an ingredient. I often cook my pasta in the skillet, transfer it to a bowl using my colander scoop or pasta spoon, drain the excess water when it is safe enough to move, rinse the skillet, and continue the recipe in the same skillet. However, feel free to cook the pasta in a stockpot, drain it, and set it aside until it's ready to use. I'm sure that most of you have more than one burner on your stove.*

Breakfast & Appetizers

My brother and I, along with half a dozen cousins, stayed with Mema every weekday in the summer months while our mothers worked. While Mema cooked three meals a day, her finest hour in the kitchen would have to be breakfast. Oh, she was the master at taking special orders.

I always requested a fried egg white—couldn't stomach the yolk then or now. One of my cousin's favorite requests was slices of cinnamon toast that he would dunk into a tall glass of strawberry-flavored milk.

And there would always be the standards already waiting on the table—hoe bread, grits, scrambled eggs, Lee smoked sausage, fresh sausage from Ratchford's market, and thick-cut bacon with chewy rinds.

When my brother was about a year old, my mama picked us up in the afternoon and found him chewing on something. She thought it was a piece of gum, but when she fished it out of his mouth, she found a piece of bacon rind he had apparently been chewing on all day long. Yes, the bacon was that good—you didn't even want to swallow it. You wanted to savor it for as long as possible.

My papa was retired but worked in his auto repair shop in the backyard. He would stop working for a while to join us for breakfast. He and my little brother would share a cup of coffee and lick peanut butter from spoons while waiting for Mema to finish cooking.

While I don't condone toddlers drinking coffee, it had no ill effects on my brother. My brother is now a grown man and in good

health. And, as Mema tells him every time she sees him, "Michael, when did you become a giant!"

If we weren't washing the food down with lukewarm coffee, strawberry milk, or gritty glasses of Tang, we were chugging glasses of Mema's extra sweet tea, a saccharin pill thrown in to increase the potency.

But my favorite part of the day was after breakfast when I would sneak back into the kitchen, grab a hunk of hoe bread, and use it to make a sandwich with whatever piece of cold, chewy breakfast meat had survived the initial onslaught of grandchildren.

After our stomachs were filled and our bloodstreams stimulated with caffeine, we went outside and played until lunch. We had no television, no video games. We didn't even take our toys there, because we couldn't trust each other not to break them. We had nothing but dirt and imagination. And it was perfect.

At my own home now, I like to cook a big breakfast on the weekends. I quickly turn into a short-order cook with a pan on every burner, coffee brewing, and orders coming in with bullet-fast speed from the three males surrounding me: seasoned hash browns, pancakes, bacon, eggs— scrambled and fried—and Texas toast on the griddle.

The meal always ends the same way with a knuckle punch between my husband and son and the ultimate compliment, "Mama makes good eggs!"

And someone always returns to the kitchen to grab the last piece of bacon.

Hunter's Hash

Although I have included three different meats in this dish, you could easily prepare this dish with one meat. In fact, you could skip the meat altogether and have a nice dish of hash browns with fried eggs. Serve it in the evening as an inexpensive breakfast for dinner.

3–4 pieces of bacon, diced	½ tsp. garlic salt
8 oz. bulk breakfast sausage	½ tsp. seasoning salt
8 oz. cooked ham, finely diced	½ tsp. pepper
8 oz. frozen diced hash brown potatoes	4–5 green onions, thinly sliced
2 Tbsp. olive oil	*Optional:* 3–4 fried eggs

1. In a large skillet, fry bacon over medium heat until crispy. Remove from skillet and set aside, retaining bacon grease.

2. Add breakfast sausage to bacon grease and cook until no pink remains.

3. Add ham to sausage mixture and cook together until ham has cooked through and browned around the edges. Remove meat from skillet and set aside.

4. In the same skillet, add hash brown potatoes and olive oil. Sprinkle with garlic salt, seasoning salt, and pepper. Cook over medium heat until hash browns have cooked through and are soft, 15–20 minutes.

5. Return all three meats to the skillet and sprinkle in green onions.

6. If including eggs in the dish, transfer hash to a large serving platter and cover with foil to keep warm while eggs are cooking. Use the skillet to fry or scramble eggs as you prefer. Place eggs on top of hash.

Serve immediately.

Hash Browns with Sausage Gravy

I always keep diced hash browns in my freezer. They are the perfect way to stretch breakfast ingredients, plus, they're one of the few breakfast foods that everyone in my family of four likes. Of course, you could always use fresh potatoes in this dish. I suggest dicing them into small pieces and boiling them for a few minutes to speed up the cooking process before adding them to the skillet.

8 oz. frozen diced hash brown potatoes

2 Tbsp. olive oil

½ tsp. garlic salt

½ tsp. seasoning salt

1 tsp. pepper, divided

8 oz. breakfast sausage

½ tsp. garlic powder

1 Tbsp. flour

2 cups milk, plus additional if needed

1. In a skillet over medium heat, add hash brown potatoes and olive oil.

2. Sprinkle in garlic salt, seasoning salt, and ½ tsp. pepper.

3. Cook until hash browns have cooked through and are soft, approximately 20 minutes. Place hash browns in a bowl and cover with foil or plastic wrap to keep warm while preparing gravy.

4. Place breakfast sausage in a skillet and cook until it is completely cooked through and no longer pink.

5. Add garlic powder, ½ tsp. pepper, and flour. Stir until flour has been absorbed completely, 3–4 minutes.

6. Slowly pour in milk and stir mixture together.

7. Leave mixture on medium-low heat for several minutes until gravy has thickened. If gravy appears too thick, add more milk and heat through.

Serve immediately over hash browns.

Bacon Fried Eggs

I checked the refrigerator one morning and found that for some strange reason I only had a few pieces of bacon left in the meat drawer. It was a strange occurrence because I always cook a whole pack of bacon at a time, so the fate of the missing bacon became an unsolved mystery. It was no mystery that my younger son was awake and asking for breakfast. I gathered up two eggs and the scant quantity of remaining bacon and whipped him up a dish that he loved and enjoys every time I make it.

2–3 pieces of bacon, diced into bite-size pieces
2 eggs
Sprinkle of salt and pepper

1. In a small skillet, cook diced bacon over medium heat until it is crisp.

2. Break the two eggs into a small bowl. Pour eggs over bacon.

3. Sprinkle with salt and pepper.

4. Cook until the eggs are cooked through, flipping halfway through the cooking process.

Serve immediately and explain that there is no more bacon available at this time.

Loaded Scrambled Eggs

So this is the dish. This is the dish that has made me famous in my home as the best breakfast cook in the world—the dish that I should take on the road and build my career around. For years, my older son claimed that he didn't eat eggs, so he would stick close to me as I cooked this dish, stopping me before I added the eggs to the skillet. "I'll just take a bowl of egg toppings, please," he'd say. In other words, he wanted ham and onions in a small bowl. I don't blame him, really. I don't eat eggs myself. Do you see the irony in this? My most "famous" dish is one that I've never tasted, but I go on faith of my family's praise that it is wonderful. One morning, my son had slept late and didn't request the egg toppings before I added the eggs. In desperation, he agreed to eat the dish "as is." He's been an egg eater ever since.

8 oz. cooked ham, finely diced

5–6 green onions, thinly sliced

1 tsp. olive oil

5–6 eggs

2 Tbsp. heavy cream, milk, or water

Sprinkle of salt, pepper, and garlic powder

1. In a medium skillet, add ham, onions, and olive oil. Cook over medium heat until onions start to soften, approximately 5 minutes.

2. In a mixing bowl, crack eggs and add liquid of your choice. Whisk together until frothy and well blended.

3. Spray sides of the skillet with cooking spray.

4. Pour eggs over ham mixture. Sprinkle with salt, pepper, and garlic powder.

5. As eggs start cooking around the sides of the skillet, use a spatula to gently pull eggs from around the skillet and fold into the middle of the skillet. Continue pulling the eggs away from the bottom and sides of the skillet until eggs have reached your desired consistency.

Serve immediately.

Hit the Road & Go Breakfast Sandwich

Some dishes hold a special place in my heart, not because I enjoy eating them, but because they take me to a certain place in time every time I prepare them. This breakfast sandwich is such a dish. I began making these sandwiches for my husband's breakfast when I was a stay-at-home mom with my two sons. My younger son was an infant who woke at 5:00 a.m. every day for the first two years of his life. Since I was up so early, I would prepare this sandwich for my husband to take with him and eat on his way to work. I became quite an expert on breakfast sandwich compilation. The yolk had to be cooked through, so it wouldn't run out and drop on my husband's shirt as he drove. I also wrapped the sandwich in wax paper and aluminum foil so it wouldn't get soggy. Adjust this sandwich to fit your taste preferences, for example, by using turkey instead of ham, excluding the cheese, or using different seasonings.

2 slices of bread

1 pat of butter or margarine

1 thick-cut slice of ham or several slices of deli ham

1 slice of your favorite cheese

1 egg

Salt and pepper to taste

1. Heat skillet to medium heat.
2. Spread butter on one side of each slice of bread. Place bread butter side down in skillet. If your skillet is small, cook bread in two batches. When bread has turned golden brown on the first side, use a spatula to flip it over to the second side. After bread has toasted slightly on second side, remove to a plate.
3. Add ham to skillet and heat through.
4. Turn one piece of bread, butter side down on a plate. Place hot ham on bread.
5. Add a slice of cheese. Set aside to allow cheese to melt.
6. Break egg into a small bowl. Spray skillet with cooking spray. Add egg and sprinkle with salt and pepper. Cook egg until it is done on both sides. Place egg on top of the cheese and cover with remaining piece of bread butter side up.
7. Cut the sandwich in half.

Serve immediately or wrap in wax paper and then in aluminum foil to eat later.

Breakfast Stacks

Breakfast is a motivational tool for me. When I feel that people in my home are acting a little sluggish and I'm ready for them to move on and start their day (away from the house), I prepare a little breakfast. They should know that in consuming the breakfast dish they are accepting that their day has begun and will commence at school and work—anywhere but here. Go, go, I've fed you. My duty is done!

1 hash brown patty

2 sausage patties

2 eggs

Sprinkle of salt and pepper

Optional: several drops of hot sauce

1. Heat a skillet over medium heat. Spray with cooking spray.

2. Add hash brown patty to skillet. Sprinkle with salt and pepper if desired. If you have room in skillet, add sausage patties. If not, cook sausage after hash brown patty. After hash brown patty has cooked through, transfer to a plate.

3. Cook sausage patties until browned and cooked through. Place on top of hash brown patty.

4. Add more cooking spray to skillet.

5. Crack eggs into a small bowl then pour into skillet. Sprinkle with salt and pepper.

6. Cook until desired level of doneness.

7. Place egg on top of sausages.

8. Add hot sauce.

Serve immediately.

Creole Shrimp Dip

I had the idea for this recipe floating around in my brain for quite a while. I imagined the ingredients coming together forming something delicious. One Saturday evening, I decided to try to bring my idea to life. We were planning on throwing some food on the grill for dinner, so I thought an appetizer would be perfect for us to munch on while waiting for the food to cook. As soon as the dish was done, my husband and I dove in, sopping it up with pieces of crusty bread. Before we knew it, the entire dish was gone; we were full, and we decided to save our planned meal for the next day.

½ red bell pepper, finely diced

½ green bell pepper, finely diced

1 small onion (or half of a large onion), finely diced

⅛ tsp. salt

¼ tsp. Creole seasoning

1 Tbsp. olive oil

12–16 oz. medium shrimp, peeled, deveined, and cut in half

1 tsp. Creole seasoning

⅛ tsp. salt

⅛ tsp. pepper

½ cup heavy whipping cream

Loaf of crusty bread

1. In a medium skillet, add bell peppers, onion, salt, and creole seasoning. Sauté in olive oil over medium heat for 10 minutes until softened. Move vegetable mixture to a small bowl, reserving any oil that remains in skillet.

2. To the same skillet, add shrimp in a single layer. Add remaining seasonings. Sauté over medium-high heat for approximately 5 minutes until shrimp are pink and cooked through.

3. Return vegetables to skillet. Lower heat to medium low and add heavy cream. Cook for 5 additional minutes until sauce is thickened.

Serve warm with crusty bread.

Hot Corn and Shrimp Dip

In my first cookbook, Southern on a Shoestring, *I included a side dish that included similar ingredients to this recipe. When I started developing recipes for this cookbook, I couldn't help but think how good those ingredients would be if they came together as a dip. I've added shrimp and cheddar cheese to the mix and served it with tortilla chips. It is a delicious improvement.*

4 slices bacon, chopped	4–5 green onions, thinly sliced
10 oz. medium shrimp, peeled, deveined, and diced	2 cups shredded cheddar cheese
8 oz. corn, thawed if using frozen corn	1 tsp. seafood seasoning
	1 tsp. hot sauce

1. In medium skillet, fry bacon until crispy. Remove bacon from skillet, reserving the grease.

2. Add shrimp to bacon grease and cook over medium heat until done, approximately 5 minutes. Remove shrimp from skillet.

3. Add corn to skillet and heat through. You may need to add a small amount of olive oil if skillet is dry.

4. Once corn is heated through, add bacon and shrimp back in, then add onions, cheese, seasoning, and hot sauce to skillet. Cook over medium heat until cheese is melted.

Serve warm with tortilla or corn chips.

Sautéed Shrimp Cocktail

Admittedly, I don't care for boiled shrimp. I don't think I've ever gone into a restaurant and ordered a shrimp cocktail. Do restaurants still offer shrimp cocktail as a selection? It seems so 1970s. In my version of shrimp cocktail, the shrimp are sautéed in a hot skillet to give them a golden crust and are served with my homemade cocktail sauce.

1 lb. shrimp, peeled and deveined

⅛ tsp. salt

⅛ tsp. pepper

½ tsp. seafood seasoning

1 Tbsp. olive oil

1. Put shrimp in medium bowl. Add salt, pepper, and seafood seasoning. Toss to coat.

2. Heat olive oil in skillet over medium-high heat. Add shrimp and cook until done, 5–6 minutes, turning shrimp during cooking process to ensure even cooking.

3. Serve warm with cocktail sauce.

Cocktail Sauce

1 cup ketchup

1–2 Tbsp. horseradish*, depending on your tastes

1 tsp. hot sauce

Juice from ½ lemon

1. Stir all ingredients together in a small bowl and refrigerate for at least 30 minutes to allow flavors to combine.

* Jars of horseradish can be found in the dairy section of your grocery store.

Deviled Crab Dip

In my home, we eat crab dishes on special occasions, such as celebrating Christmas holidays or developing recipes for a cookbook. So this dish is special to me because it reminds me of the small things that families do to make the holidays their own. For us, it is having a nice warm crab dish that we can savor together while discussing our holiday plans.

8 oz. cream cheese, softened	⅛ tsp. pepper
2 Tbsp. dijon-style mustard	½ tsp. hot sauce
1 tsp. seafood seasoning	8 oz. crab
½ tsp. garlic salt	4 green onions, thinly sliced
½ tsp. paprika	Additional paprika for garnish

1. In large mixing bowl, add cream cheese, mustard, seasonings, and hot sauce. Stir together until completely blended.

2. Gently stir in crab and green onions to prevent breaking up crab too much.

3. Spread mixture in a skillet and cook over medium heat until warm and bubbly.

4. Sprinkle with paprika.

Serve warm with crackers.

Vidalia Onion & Clam Dip

I cannot stress to you the pleasure I get in smelling onions frying in a skillet. It consumes the senses, the kitchen, and the home. People will come out of the woodwork, or at least their bedrooms, to investigate what's cooking. Frying onions is the perfect start to so many delicious dishes. This dip puts a different spin on onion dip, and I think it's best after chilling in the refrigerator overnight.

2 large vidalia onions (or other sweet onions), thinly sliced

1 Tbsp. olive oil

½ tsp. pepper

½ tsp. salt

½ tsp. garlic powder

½ tsp. garlic salt

½ tsp. onion powder

1 Tbsp. balsamic vinegar

2 (6.5 oz.) cans chopped clams, drained with juice reserved

16 oz. sour cream

1. In large skillet, add onions and olive oil. Cook over medium heat until onions are soft and golden brown, approximately 30 minutes, stirring frequently.

2. When onions are cooked, add seasonings, vinegar, clams, and ¼ cup of the clam juice. Cook for another 5 minutes or so until clam liquid is cooked off. Cool mixture completely.

3. After mixture is cooled, stir in sour cream. Refrigerate until completely cold.

Serve with crackers or tortilla chips.

Jalapeño Poppers Dip

You're never too old to learn something new about yourself and your taste preferences. I avoided jalapenos for years because I thought they were too hot. But I've found that if I completely remove all of the seeds and veins that they're actually fairly mild. I can enjoy the flavor of the pepper without suffering from the heat. If you like heat, leave the seeds and veins in when you're preparing the dish. I suggest reduced-fat cheeses to decrease the oil in this dip.

7–8 jalapeño peppers, deseeded, deveined, and sliced

8 oz. bulk sausage

1 cup reduced-fat mozzarella cheese

1 cup reduced-fat cheddar cheese

5 slices bacon, cooked and chopped

1 Tbsp. ranch dressing mix

1. Prepare jalapeños by cutting in half and deseeding, deveining, and slicing into small pieces. Set aside.

2. In skillet, cook sausage over medium heat until cooked through. Drain excess grease if necessary.

3. Add jalapeños and cook until peppers have softened.

4. Add cheeses and stir until melted.

5. Sprinkle in bacon and dressing mix and cook until mixture is bubbly.

Serve warm with tortilla chips.

Cocktail Sausages in Savory Sauce

Have you ever been to a gathering where there wasn't a slow cooker full of cocktail sausages simmering away in a sauce of grape jelly and chili sauce? Yeah, me neither. They're a classic because they're delicious and familiar. Never underestimate the power of familiar food. It draws people like bees to nectar. This recipe easily doubles or triples depending on how many people you're trying to attract. You can also throw all of the ingredients into a slow cooker if that's your thing.

¼ cup honey

¼ cup mustard-style barbecue sauce

1 Tbsp. sriracha sauce

14 oz. cocktail smoked sausages

1. In a small bowl, blend honey, barbecue sauce, and sriracha sauce. Set aside.

2. Add sausages to a skillet and cover with sauce blend. Heat over medium-low heat for approximately 10 minutes until sauce is bubbly and sausages are heated through.

Serve warm with crackers.

Georgia Peach Pork Meatballs

With this recipe I wanted to put a Southern twist on the more traditional meatballs and pineapple dish by substituting peaches for the pineapples. While I used peach preserves, you can substitute apricot preserves since that may be more readily available. You can also substitute frozen, thawed peaches for fresh peaches.

Meatballs:
- 1 lb. ground pork
- 1 cup plain bread crumbs
- ½ tsp. salt
- 2 Tbsp. peach preserves
- 1 Tbsp. olive oil

Sauce:
- 1 peach, peeled and diced
- ½ cup mustard-style barbecue sauce
- ¼ cup peach preserves
- 1 Tbsp. maple syrup
- 1 Tbsp. brown sugar

1. In a bowl, mix together pork, bread crumbs, salt, and preserves. Shape into 1" meatballs.

2. Heat olive oil in a skillet. Add meatballs and cook over medium heat, browning all sides of meatballs, turning frequently and carefully. When meatballs are golden brown on all sides, remove from skillet and set aside.

3. Mix all sauce ingredients together in a small bowl.

4. Add sauce ingredients to skillet and bring to a simmer.

5. Return meatballs to skillet and simmer for approximately 10 minutes until meatballs are cooked through.

Serve warm with crusty bread.

Smoky Pulled Pork Spinach Dip

This dish is the perfect way to use up leftover pulled pork, if there is such a thing. I will confess that I took a shortcut with this dip by stopping by my local BBQ joint and picking up a pound of pulled pork. Don't worry—the excess didn't go to waste.

4 pieces bacon, cooked and chopped

1 cup pulled pork

8 oz. fresh baby spinach

½ tsp. liquid smoke

¼ tsp. pepper

¼ cup heavy cream

½ cup parmesan cheese

1. Cook bacon in skillet until crispy. Remove from skillet and set aside, reserving bacon grease.

2. Add pulled pork to bacon grease and heat through.

3. Add spinach, liquid smoke, and pepper to pork mixture. Cook until spinach is wilted.

4. Add heavy cream and parmesan cheese, cooking until cheese is melted.

5. Sprinkle in cooked bacon.

Serve warm with tortilla chips or crusty bread.

Boneless Wing Dip

This recipe is what I consider to be a good starting point for chicken dip. The basic recipe lends itself to an endless variety of dips because you can add your preferred ingredients. You can serve it warm, room temperature, or cold. It's a versatile recipe that can be changed each time you make it.

1–2 boneless chicken breasts

Sprinkle of garlic salt
    and pepper

1 tsp. olive oil

1 Tbsp. butter

1 Tbsp. hot sauce

2–3 green onions, thinly sliced

Optional add-ins:

8 oz. sour cream

8 oz. cream cheese

16 oz. shredded cheddar cheese

1. Sprinkle chicken with garlic salt and pepper.

2. Add olive oil to a skillet and cook chicken over medium heat until cooked through.

3. Take chicken out of skillet and, using two forks, shred chicken and return to skillet.

4. Add butter and hot sauce and cook until bubbly.

5. Sprinkle in green onions.

At this point, you may cool the mixture completely and add your preference of sour cream, cream cheese, or cheddar cheese or a combination of the three for a cold dip. You may also add these ingredients to the warm mixture and serve warm with tortilla chips.

Three Pepper Chicken Dip

"Does anyone want any of this chicken dip that I made for the cookbook? It's got a little kick to it." I took the silence that followed my question as a lack of interest on the part of my family. Good! That's how I wanted it in the first place. I sat down on the couch with a bag of tortilla scoops and consumed almost the entire dish, occasionally asking my husband if he wanted to try it while secretly hoping his answer was no. It's that good!

2 boneless chicken breasts, diced

1 Tbsp. olive oil

Sprinkle of salt and pepper

3 jalapeños, deveined, deseeded, and sliced

1 red bell pepper, diced

1 Tbsp. hot sauce

¼ cup heavy cream

4 slices reduced-fat provolone cheese

1. Place chicken and olive oil in a skillet over medium heat. Add salt and pepper. Cook until chicken is cooked through. Remove chicken from skillet and set aside.

2. Add jalapeños and bell pepper to skillet and cook until softened, 8–10 minutes.

3. Return chicken to skillet.

4. Add hot sauce and cream.

5. Once cream is heated through, add cheese. Cook until cheese is melted and stir to combine all ingredients.

Serve warm with tortilla chips.

Marinara Meatballs

You may not be aware of this, but appetizers have siblings. Please meet the sister of the cocktail sausage, Marinara. It's very rare that they attend a party without each other. You will often see Marinara acting as Smokey's wingman. She'll draw you over to her with her enticing aroma, and while you're admiring her beautiful ruby sauce with basil accents, she'll whisper in your ear, "Have you met my brother? He's a good guy. His name is Smokey and he's right over there relaxing in the hot tub. He would love to meet you." Before you know it, your plate is full of cocktail sausages and meatballs. You'll eat more than you should and you might feel a little ashamed of yourself afterward. But, oh, what memories you'll have!

1 lb. ground beef	¼ tsp. Italian seasoning
½ cup Italian bread crumbs	1 Tbsp. olive oil
½ tsp. garlic salt	1 cup marinara sauce
½ tsp. garlic powder	2 Tbsp. fresh basil, finely chopped

1. In a mixing bowl, combine ground beef, bread crumbs, garlic salt, garlic powder, and Italian seasoning. Shape into one-inch meatballs.

2. Heat olive oil in a skillet over medium heat. Add meatballs and brown on all sides, turning frequently and carefully.

3. Add marinara sauce and lower heat to medium-low. Let simmer for approximately 10 minutes until meatballs are cooked through.

4. Sprinkle basil over meatballs before serving.

Serve with crusty bread.

Pepper Steak Dip

One of my hobbies is perusing meat departments in grocery stores looking for marked down meat. My daddy was a meat cutter until he retired, and he told me that beef was the safest bet when it comes to buying meat that has been marked down. Although I often see sales stickers on pork and chicken, I just stick to beef. I'll often find a single steak marked down and will buy it and stick it in my freezer. I don't necessarily have a plan for it, but I'll figure something out eventually. I wouldn't dare grill one steak and call it a meal for the four of us; however, I've found that I can stretch a steak by cutting it into bite-size pieces and using it in stir-fries and dishes such as this one.

2 green bell peppers, thinly sliced

2 Tbsp. olive oil, divided

1 large onion, thinly sliced

1 pinch of salt

1 lb. steak (rib eye, skirt, or chuck steak), thinly sliced and diced

½ tsp. garlic salt

½ tsp. pepper

1 Tbsp. Worcestershire sauce

1 Tbsp. soy sauce

4 slices reduced-fat provolone cheese

1. In skillet, add bell peppers and one tablespoon of olive oil. Sauté on medium-high heat for 5 minutes.

2. Add sliced onions to the mixture. Add a pinch of salt and cook until vegetables have caramelized around the edges. Remove from skillet and set aside.

3. Add another tablespoon of olive oil to the pan. Add steak, garlic salt, and pepper. Sauté steak until browned and cooked through. Cooking time will vary based on the thickness of meat slices.

4. Add Worcestershire and soy sauces. Lower heat to medium-low, cover skillet, and cook steak mixture for 10 minutes.

5. Uncover and add pepper and onion mixture to the skillet.

6. Place cheese on top of mixture and allow it to melt over steak.

Serve warm with crusty bread.

Pepperoni Pizza Bread

This bread should be cooked on low heat to prevent the bottom from burning. If you prefer, you can prepare this dish and heat it in a toaster oven. Serve this bread with a bowl of warm marinara sauce.

1 Tbsp. butter, softened

¼ tsp. garlic powder

1 small loaf of bread such as sourdough, Italian bread, or French bread (choose bread that will fit into your skillet)

¼ cup parmesan cheese

¼ cup mini pepperoni or diced pepperoni

1. In small bowl, mix together butter and garlic powder. Set aside.

2. Slice loaf of bread in half to form an open-face loaf. Cut the loaf to fit in your skillet if necessary.

3. Heat dry skillet over medium heat.

4. Spread butter mixture over open face of bread and place facedown in heated skillet.

5. Using a spatula, check progress of bread. This process will take only 1–2 minutes. When bread has reached your desired toastiness, turn bread over and lower heat to low.

6. Sprinkle cheese evenly over two pieces of bread. Place pepperoni on bread.

7. Cover skillet and allow cheese to melt over bread and pepperoni to heat through, 3–4 minutes.

8. Cut into strips for serving.

Apple Pie Dip

Let me confess something to you. After I made the pecan topping for this dish, I ate some of it. I called myself testing it, but one piece lead to another. I could have eaten the entire batch and I almost did. However, I'm glad that I did save enough to go into the apple mixture. The flavors blended well together. While I'm suggesting you serve it with crackers, I actually ate it with a spoon.

Pecan topping:

½ cup pecans, finely chopped

2 Tbsp. brown sugar

2 Tbsp. butter

Apple mixture:

4 medium apples, cored, peeled and diced

½ cup brown sugar

¼ tsp. cinnamon

1 tsp. vanilla

Juice of 1 lemon

1 Tbsp. butter

Pecan topping:

1. In medium skillet, bring pecans, brown sugar, and butter to a boil over medium heat. Cook 3–4 minutes.

2. Spread pecan mixture on a plate lined with wax paper to cool while preparing apple mixture.

Apple mixture:

1. In a medium skillet, add apples, brown sugar, cinnamon, vanilla, lemon juice, and butter.

2. Cook over medium-low heat until apples are soft and sauce has thickened, approximately 30 minutes.

3. Let cool slightly before adding pecan mixture.

Serve warm or at room temperature with cinnamon graham crackers or pita crisps.

Pecan Pie Dip

My husband loves pecan pie. I usually make him one around the Thanksgiving holiday. My husband also loves to enjoy his pie behind my back, like after I've gone to bed at night. I only tell you this because the fact that I'm not there to supervise his consumption of pie is what led to the idea for this dish. Whenever I would go to the refrigerator to cut myself a piece of pie, I would find that my husband had only eaten the filling of the pie, leaving the crust intact. So even though I thought there was pie, there was only an empty shell of what used to be pie. I decided to do away with the shell altogether by making the filling in a skillet. No more disappointment.

3 large eggs

1 cup sugar

¾ cup light corn syrup

1 stick margarine, melted

1 tsp. vanilla extract

¼ tsp. salt

1½ cups pecans, finely chopped

1. In large mixing bowl, add eggs and sugar. Stir until completely blended.

2. Add corn syrup and melted margarine. Stir until blended.

3. Stir in vanilla, salt, and pecans.

4. Pour mixture into a medium skillet. Cover tightly with foil.

5. Cook on low heat for 30–35 minutes. Remove from heat. The mixture will set as it cools.

Serve with graham crackers or shortbread cookies, or eat with a spoon after your spouse goes to bed.

Side Dishes

The Comfort of Others

Sometimes I can be funny, nay, witty. Witty is like funny, but with some brains behind it. I don't say witty things to be the center of attention. Actually, I don't want attention at all. My wit is a survival mechanism. If I can make people laugh, they will feel more comfortable around me. Once people are more comfortable around me, I can withdraw into the background without anyone noticing. As with most introverts, the background is where I thrive.

I use food in much the same way as I use wit, as a survival mechanism. Feeding people works on two levels: the basic of needing food to survive, and the complexity of feeding people to make them more comfortable. We use food to celebrate and to mourn. I use food to communicate. What I cannot say in words, I say in food. "I made you a pound cake," actually means, "I love you. You're my best friend. Don't ever leave me." You had me at pound cake.

There is a payoff for feeding others, whether or not I'm present to watch them eat the food that I have prepared. That payoff is a feeling of satisfying accomplishment that, for at least a few minutes in time, I was able to provide someone with comfort. If at the end of it all I'm only remembered as the funny lady who could cook well, then my life has been a success.

Pico de Gallo Rice

It's hard to believe that there was a time when I didn't eat pico de gallo. My friend Judith introduced me to it. She shared her order with me one day while we were out at lunch. I fell in love with it and started ordering my own bowl whenever we would go out for lunch. On one occasion, the cook must have stubbed his toe with the salt. The pico was so salty that we could barely eat. We continued to eat the pico despite the level of saltiness and prayed that the mistake would never be made again. That mistake hasn't happened since, but I keep my fingers crossed every time. The restaurant where we ate didn't have jalapenos in their pico, so I don't include them in mine. Feel free to do so if you'd like.

Pico de Gallo:

3 plum tomatoes, deseeded and finely diced

¼ red onion, finely diced

¼ cup cilantro, finely diced

Juice of one lime

⅛ tsp. salt

Rice:

1 cup rice

1 Tbsp. olive oil

1 tsp. salt

¼ tsp. garlic powder

½ tsp. ground cumin

2 cups chicken broth

Half of the pico de gallo

Pico de Gallo:

1. In small bowl, combine all ingredients. Set aside. May be made ahead and refrigerated until ready to use.

Rice:

1. Add rice and olive oil to skillet. Sauté over medium-high heat until rice is coated with olive oil.

2. Add salt, garlic powder, and cumin. Stir until rice is coated with seasonings.

3. Add chicken broth and half of the pico de gallo. Bring to boil. Cover skillet and reduce heat to low.

4. Cook 15–20 minutes until all liquid is absorbed. Fluff with a fork.

5. Add remaining pico de gallo to the rice before serving.

Serve with chicken or Mexican dishes.

Nutty Rice Pilaf

I keep searching the job listings in my local newspaper to see if there are any openings for nut toasters in my area. So far, I've come up with nothing. But I have to tell you that I'm really good at it. The restaurants around here don't know what they're missing by not hiring me to toast nuts. I love the process of toasting nuts, from the care given to not burning the nuts to the intoxicating smell of the nuts toasting in the skillet. If you haven't toasted nuts, do it. But make sure you're ready to commit to the process—serious applicants only.

½ cup slivered almonds, toasted

½ cup orzo

½ cup rice

1 Tbsp. olive oil

2 cups chicken broth

1 tsp. salt

½ tsp. garlic powder

1. To toast almonds, heat dry skillet over medium heat. Add almonds and toast until golden brown, 7–8 minutes, stirring often. Do not leave almonds unattended—they can burn fairly quickly. Once almonds are toasted, remove from the heat and set aside.

2. In a medium skillet, add the orzo, rice, and olive oil. Cook over medium-high heat until orzo begins to toast to a golden brown, 5–6 minutes.

3. Add chicken broth, salt, garlic powder, and toasted almonds.

4. Bring to boil and cover. Lower heat to low and cook until rice is fluffy and liquid has been absorbed, 18–20 minutes.

5. Fluff with fork to distribute the almonds.

Serve with chicken or pork dishes.

Beefy Onion Rice

Over the years, I have pretty much eliminated any need to buy flavored boxed rice mixes. I've worked on different flavor combinations that cover almost every flavor available in the grocery store. My husband will often ask what brand of rice we're eating and I explain that I made the rice from scratch. I prefer to use jasmine rice over long-grain rice. It makes for a fluffier and more flavorful rice dish.

½ cup onions, finely diced

1 Tbsp. butter

1 tsp. beef bouillon granules

1 tsp. soy sauce

½ tsp. onion powder

½ tsp. salt

⅛ tsp. pepper

1 cup rice

2 cups beef broth

1. Add onions and butter to a skillet and cook over medium heat until onions are soft and translucent.

2. Add beef bouillon granules, soy sauce, onion powder, salt, and pepper and stir until dissolved in butter mixture.

3. Add rice and beef broth.

4. Bring to boil and cover. Lower heat to low and cook until rice is fluffy and liquid has been absorbed, 18–20 minutes.

5. Fluff with fork before serving.

Serve with beef or pork dishes.

Lemon & Herb Rice

If you've never zested a lemon, add it to your bucket list. Buy yourself a zester and a lemon and set aside some private time to take a sensory vacation right in your own kitchen. Watch as the yellow specks drop into the bowl. Bring the bowl to your nose and inhale one of the most wonderful scents that nature has to offer. Now, rub your fingers together and feel the oil from the zest spread over them. Close your eyes and bring your fingers to your nose. Inhale deeply and know that life is good.

Zest of two lemons

½ cup fresh parsley, chopped

1 cup rice

1 Tbsp. olive oil

1 tsp. salt

2 cups water

1. In small bowl, combine lemon zest and parsley. Set aside.

2. In skillet, combine rice and olive oil. Stir over medium-high heat until rice is coated with olive oil.

3. Add salt.

4. Add water and half of lemon and parsley mixture.

5. Bring rice to boil, cover skillet, and lower heat. Cook 15–20 minutes until liquid is absorbed.

6. Fluff rice with a fork and add remaining lemon mixture.

Serve with chicken or seafood dishes.

Traditional Yellow Rice

Saffron is not a cheap ingredient. I'll go ahead and tell you that up front. I paid several dollars for a tiny plastic box filled with precious strands of saffron. I kept the box tucked away in my cupboard like a cherished family heirloom. Did I dare use it? No, it was too expensive. I had to save it for hard times. Because when times get hard, how often do you wish you had saffron to ease your troubled mind? So in a moment of carpe diem, I chose to knock the dust of my box of saffron and see what all the excitement was about. While saffron doesn't have a distinct flavor, when combined with the flavors included here, it creates a beautiful yellow rice dish.

1 cup rice	¼ tsp. turmeric
1 Tbsp. olive oil	8–10 strands saffron
1 tsp. salt	2 cups chicken broth
½ tsp. garlic powder	

1. In skillet over medium-high heat, add rice and olive oil. Stir together until rice is coated with oil.

2. Add salt, garlic powder, turmeric, and saffron. Stir until rice is coated with seasonings.

3. Pour in chicken broth.

4. Bring mixture to a boil. Cover skillet and lower heat to low. Cook 15–20 minutes until liquid is absorbed.

5. Fluff with fork before serving.

Serve with chicken, pork, or seafood dishes.

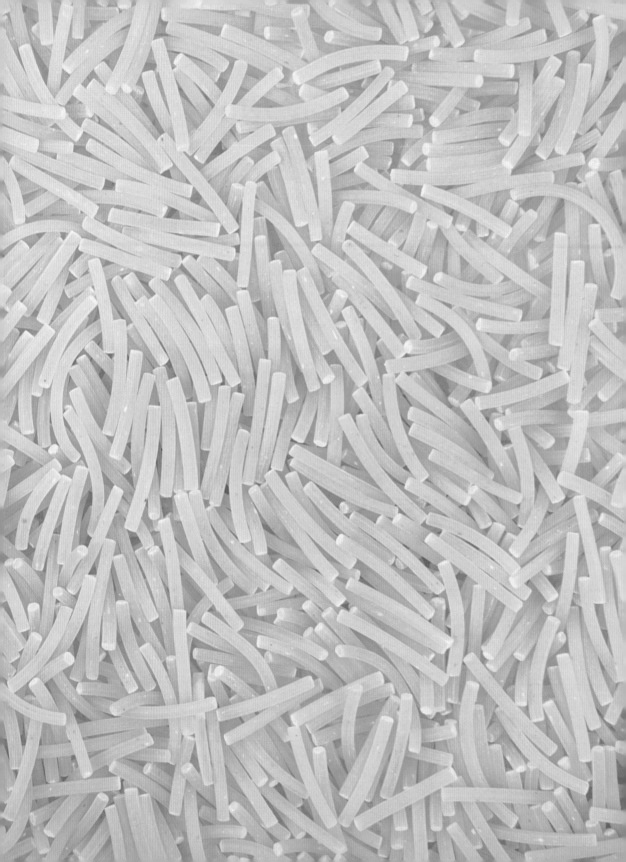

The Story of Seasoned Noodles

When I told my sons that I was writing my first cookbook, the first thing they asked was if I would be including the recipe for seasoned noodles. They were greatly disappointed to learn that I would not be including an entry for seasoned noodles. With this cookbook, I feel that, even though the dish would not be considered worthy as an official recipe for most readers, it is worthy of mention for the sake of my sons and the memories that the dish elicits for them.

Here is the story of how seasoned noodles came to be. My oldest son was eighteen months old before he cut any teeth. His first tooth was a molar, so his diet consisted of a lot of soft, mushy foods that didn't require a lot of chewing. Rice and pasta were his favorite dishes.

My husband worked away from home most of the time, so my son and I were alone together for most meals. I wanted to cook a meal that we could both eat. I don't eat bland food and didn't believe that my child should eat bland food either. So I would cook vermicelli noodles, drain them, then drizzle them with olive oil and garlic salt. I don't know at what point these noodles came to be known as seasoned noodles, but I do know that my son loved them and ate them daily for years. Even now, as a teenager, his face lights up when he sees me making them for him.

Not only did he eat these noodles at home, he also expected to eat them anywhere he went, including restaurants and relatives' homes. Imagine the look on a server's face when a child would tell her, "I'll take seasoned noodles." My mom even had to buy a bottle of olive oil for her kitchen so she could whip this dish up for him whenever he was there long enough to eat a meal.

At one point, my son was sick and had to miss school. I had to leave him with my in-laws one day since I was working outside of the home. While sitting at my desk at work, I received a phone call from my husband's eighty-year-old stepmother, D, asking me what seasoned noodles were.

Me: "Do you have any long noodles like spaghetti?"
D: "Yes."
Me: "Do you have olive oil?"
D: "Yes"
Me: "Do you have garlic salt?"
D: "Yes."
Me: "That's what he wants. Cook the noodles, drain them, then drizzle with olive oil, and sprinkle with garlic salt."

Savory Chicken Noodles

Even though D is no longer in our lives, my son says, "I don't remember much about her, but I do remember that she made pretty good seasoned noodles." And now, you can too.

While browsing through the ethnic food aisle at my local grocery store, my attention was caught by a small package of pasta. It was called fideo, a finely chopped Mexican pasta, the equivalent of vermicelli. I have several grocery stores in my area and all of them carry it. Fideo is great for soups and for this recipe. If you can't find fideo pasta, just break up vermicelli into bite-size pieces.

2 cups water

1 Tbsp. butter or margarine

2 chicken bouillon cubes

½ tsp. garlic powder

½ tsp. dried parsley

¼ tsp. paprika

8 oz. of vermicelli, broken into 1-inch pieces or 7 oz. package of fideo pasta (from Mexican food section)

1. Place all ingredients except pasta in medium skillet and bring to boil.

2. Add pasta.

3. Lower heat to medium-low and cook uncovered until most of the liquid has been absorbed, 6–7 minutes, stirring occasionally to prevent noodles from sticking together. Remove from heat. Noodles will thicken upon standing.

Serve immediately as a meal or as a side for chicken dishes.

Savory Beef Noodles

For years I've purchased those envelope packets of noodles in sauce. While these packets are inexpensive, they just don't contain enough food to feed my family of four, even as a side dish. I've developed this dish that I like even more than the packets. You can add cooked vegetables or meat to turn it into a main dish.

2 cups water

1 Tbsp. butter or margarine

2 beef bouillon cubes

½ tsp. garlic powder

½ tsp. dried parsley

¼ tsp. pepper

8 oz. of vermicelli, broken into 1-inch pieces or 7 oz. package of fideo pasta (from Mexican food section)

1. Place all ingredients except pasta in medium skillet and bring to boil.

2. Add pasta.

3. Lower heat to medium-low and cook uncovered until most of the liquid has been absorbed, 6–7 minutes, stirring occasionally to prevent noodles from sticking together. Remove from heat. Noodles will thicken upon standing.

Serve immediately as a meal or as a side dish for beef or pork dishes.

Asparagus Casserole Skillet

After I graduated from college, I worked as a secretary in the school's biology department. We would have a potluck gathering before Christmas break each year. One of the professors brought in an asparagus casserole. He called it his specialty. It was the equivalent of green bean casserole with mushy, canned asparagus substituted for canned green beans. While I find frozen asparagus to be a suitable substitute for fresh asparagus in some dishes, I do not condone the use of canned asparagus under any circumstances. Even though I didn't like his casserole, the idea of an asparagus casserole appealed to me and I tucked the idea away for future reference. It was over twenty years before I pulled it out of the archives of my brain and brought it to life in my skillet. It was worth the wait.

---

1 cup panko bread crumbs, toasted

2 bunches asparagus (approximately 2 lbs.)

2 Tbsp. olive oil

½ tsp. salt

¼ tsp. pepper

1 onion, thinly sliced

Pinch of salt and pepper

½ cup finely chopped mushrooms

½ cup chicken or beef broth

1 Tbsp. Worcestershire sauce

1 Tbsp. soy sauce

1 tsp. balsamic vinegar

¼ cup heavy cream

---

1. In dry skillet over medium heat, add bread crumbs. Stir frequently to ensure even toasting and to prevent burning. Remove bread crumbs from heat when they're golden brown, after 7–8 minutes. Set aside until ready to use.

2. Remove woody ends from asparagus and cut remaining stalks into bite-size pieces.

3. In large skillet, add asparagus, olive oil, salt, and pepper. Cook over medium heat for approximately 10 minutes, stirring frequently. Remove the asparagus from the skillet and set aside.

4. Add onions and a pinch of salt and pepper. Add more olive oil if skillet is too dry. Cook the onions until soft and translucent, 5–6 minutes.

5. Add mushrooms to onions and cook together until mushrooms are soft, approximately 10 minutes.

6. Return asparagus to skillet.

7. Add chicken broth, Worcestershire sauce, soy sauce, and balsamic vinegar. Bring to boil and allow to reduce for approximately 5 minutes.

8. Add heavy cream and let mixture heat through and reduce another 5 minutes.

9. Turn off heat and sprinkle bread crumbs on top of dish. Allow mixture to cool slightly and let bread crumbs absorb some of the liquid.

Serve immediately with chicken or pork dishes.

Squash & Onions

There is nothing more exciting than picking the first squash of the season. You just look at it and imagine the possibilities. By the end of the growing season, your enthusiasm wanes a bit. What can you possibly do with it that you haven't already done? While I use squash in casseroles, my favorite way is to simply cook it with onions. I love to get the squash caramelized around the edges. It is wonderful!

1 Tbsp. olive oil	½ tsp. salt
1 onion, finely chopped	¼ tsp. pepper
3 medium squash, sliced	⅛ tsp. poultry seasoning

1. Place all ingredients in large skillet.

2. Cook over medium heat for 15 minutes or until squash reaches desired doneness and excess liquid is absorbed.

Serve as a side for chicken or pork dishes.

The Story of Hibachi at Home

My husband and I met on a blind date. That first night, we ate at a Japanese steakhouse and, through the years, we returned to that restaurant quite often. After we got married, we imagined what it would be like to one day take our future children to the same restaurant. Would they enjoy it like we did? Our future children finally arrived and they loved nothing more than to go out to dinner and watch the hibachi chefs in action.

After a while, our favorite restaurant closed and we had to move our base of operation to the newer Japanese restaurant in town. Two things happened: this restaurant was more expensive than the first, and the boys were no longer satisfied with kids' meals. So a fairly expensive meal became an extremely expensive meal. It also became a special occasion meal, as in we only go twice a year to celebrate the end of the school year and to celebrate the boys' birthdays, which are, fortunately for my budget, a day apart.

My husband and I decided that we needed to replicate the meal at home. I made a jar of ginger dressing for the salad. I searched the Internet for a copycat recipe of our favorite condiment, shrimp sauce. I fried a large amount of rice in the skillet. I also sautéed shrimp and steak, smothered in soy sauce and butter. As a side for the rice, I whipped up these hibachi-style zucchini and onions. The meal was a success in the eyes of all, and some of those eyes are picky.

Hibachi-Style Zucchini & Onions

1 Tbsp. sesame seeds, toasted

1 large onion, cut into wedges

2 Tbsp. olive oil

3 medium zucchini, cut into wedges

1/8 tsp. salt

1/8 tsp. pepper

1 tsp. soy sauce

1. To toast sesame seeds, begin with a dry skillet. Pour the seeds into the skillet and place over medium heat. As skillet begins to heat up, the seeds will start to toast. This will happen quickly, so do not walk away during this process. Stir the seeds frequently to avoid burning. As soon as the seeds start to turn golden brown (4–5 minutes), remove them from the heat and pour into a small bowl until you are ready to use them.

2. Add the onions and olive oil to the skillet. Cook for 2–3 minutes on medium-high heat.

3. Add the zucchini and continue cooking the mixture until the vegetables have caramelized and softened, 6–8 minutes.

4. Sprinkle in the salt and pepper and add the soy sauce.

5. After the soy sauce has reduced, sprinkle in the sesame seeds.

Serve immediately with rice, shrimp, and steak for a Japanese steakhouse feast.

Garlic Mashed Potatoes

When my budget is tight, I know that I can always turn to my old friend, the potato, to help me out by providing a hearty and filling side dish. I don't know what I or meat loaf would do without him.

2 lbs. potatoes, cubed	1 cup heavy whipping cream
1 Tbsp. salt	1 tsp. garlic salt
5–6 garlic cloves	¼ tsp. salt
1 stick of butter, softened	¼ tsp. pepper

1. In large skillet, add potatoes, salt, and garlic cloves.

2. Cover with water and bring to boil. Cook until potatoes are soft and tender. Cooking time will vary based on size of potatoes.

3. When potatoes are done, carefully drain them and return mixture to skillet.

4. Add butter, cream, and seasonings. Using potato masher, blend all ingredients together. Taste for seasoning. Add more if necessary.

Serve immediately with chicken or beef dishes.

Skillet Scalloped Potatoes

Oh, I do love a good scalloped potato; even the boxed meal can be snazzed up to become something delicious. I love it when the potatoes start to cool off and the sauce thickens. I've never had to put leftover scalloped potatoes in the refrigerator. I always finish off the pan when no one is looking. These potatoes lend themselves to add-ins such as onions, chives, cheese, bacon, and ham.

---

1 lb. small potatoes, thinly sliced

⅓ cup flour

1 tsp. garlic salt

½ tsp. pepper

3 Tbsp. butter, diced into small pieces

1 cup heavy whipping cream

---

1. Thinly slice potatoes and keep in bowl of cold water to prevent browning until ready to use. When ready to use, pat dry with paper towel.

2. In small bowl, combine flour, garlic salt, and pepper. Set aside.

3. Spray medium skillet with cooking spray.

4. Add single, even layer of potato slices, approximately ⅓ of the potatoes. Sprinkle ⅓ flour mixture over potatoes. Add ⅓ of the diced butter. Repeat layers until all ingredients are used.

5. Pour whipping cream over potatoes.

6. Cover skillet tightly with foil.

7. Cook over medium-low heat for approximately 20 minutes. Remove foil and carefully fold potatoes from bottom to top. Continue cooking uncovered until potatoes are done, testing frequently to check for doneness.

Serve immediately with chicken or pork dishes.

Green Bean Casserole Skillet

I work hard to make more and more dishes from scratch. Green bean casserole is one of those dishes that is easily converted to scratch ingredients. The sauce in this dish will thicken as it cools. Delicious!

1 lb. fresh green beans, trimmed, cut in half

4–5 slices bacon, diced

½ onion, finely diced

¼ tsp. salt

¼ tsp. pepper

½ tsp. onion powder

½ tsp. garlic powder

1 cup chicken broth

½ cup heavy cream

1 tsp. soy sauce

1 Tbsp. butter

1. Prepare green beans by trimming ends and cutting in half. Set aside.

2. Cook bacon in large skillet over medium heat until crispy. Add onions and cook until translucent. Remove bacon and onions from skillet and set aside, reserving bacon grease in skillet.

3. Add beans to bacon grease in skillet. Sprinkle with salt, pepper, onion powder, and garlic powder. Stir until beans are coated with seasonings, cooking on medium heat for approximately 5 minutes.

4. Add chicken broth and cook until most of the broth has reduced, 10–12 minutes.

5. Add heavy cream and soy sauce and cook until mixture thickens and coats the green beans, 6–7 minutes.

6. Add butter and cook for an additional 2–3 minutes until butter has melted.

7. Return bacon and onion mixture to dish and stir to fully incorporate.

8. Sauce will thicken as mixture cools.

Serve with pork or beef dishes.

Teriyaki Green Beans

I only purchase three types of canned vegetables: corn, tomatoes, and green beans. This recipe is the perfect way to doctor up canned green beans and turn them into something special.

2 slices bacon, diced

1 onion, finely diced

2 (14.5 oz.) cans cut
    green beans, drained

1 Tbsp. teriyaki sauce

1 Tbsp. soy sauce

¼ tsp. pepper

Salt to taste

1. Cook bacon in skillet over medium-high heat until crisp. Remove bacon from skillet and set aside, reserving bacon grease.

2. Add onions to bacon grease, and cook on medium heat until caramelized, approximately 10 minutes.

3. Add green beans, sauces, and seasonings and simmer over medium heat for approximately 10 minutes.

4. Sprinkle with bacon.

Serve immediately with chicken or beef dishes.

Lemon Pepper Broccoli

Broccoli is the universal vegetable in our home, the one vegetable that I can count on all four of us to eat. This dish cooks up quickly and everyone loves it.

10 oz. fresh broccoli florets

1 Tbsp. olive oil

Zest of one lemon

¼ tsp. lemon pepper

Salt to taste

1. If using a whole head of broccoli, cut into bite-size florets and set aside.

2. In large skillet, heat olive oil over medium heat.

3. Add broccoli and cook until it reaches desired tenderness, stirring frequently and carefully throughout cooking process.

4. When broccoli has reached your desired tenderness, add lemon zest, lemon pepper, and salt.

Serve immediately with fish or chicken dishes.

Spicy Red Pepper Cauliflower

I often forget that I like cauliflower. I rarely buy it because I never seem to notice it in the grocery store. Maybe it is because my eyes are drawn to the beautiful greens, reds, and yellows of the produce section. But every now and then, for no particular reason, I'll just blurt out, "I like cauliflower." So here we are.

1 red bell pepper, finely diced

1 Tbsp. olive oil

1 head cauliflower, cut into
    bite-size pieces

¼ tsp. salt

Pinch of red pepper flakes

1. In large skillet, add bell pepper and olive oil. Cook over medium heat for 8–10 minutes until soft. Remove peppers from skillet.

2. Add cauliflower to skillet. If skillet appears dry, add a little more olive oil.

3. Sprinkle salt and red pepper flakes on cauliflower. Cook cauliflower until desired tenderness, 8–10 minutes.

4. Return bell peppers back to the dish and stir through until evenly distributed.

Serve immediately with chicken or beef dishes.

Loaded Corn Cakes

If you have a scratch cornbread recipe that you like, feel free to use it here instead of a boxed mix. You can also add some cheese to the batter.

1 (7.5 oz.) package cornbread or corn muffin mix plus ingredients listed on package

¼ tsp. pepper

¼ tsp. seasoning salt

¼ tsp. garlic powder

3 green onions, finely chopped

¼ green or red bell pepper, finely chopped

¼ cup corn

1. Prepare mix according to package directions.

2. Add pepper, seasoning salt, and garlic powder.

3. Stir in green onions, bell pepper, and corn.

4. Heat skillet over medium heat. Spray with cooking spray.

5. Drop batter by ¼ cup at a time into skillet.

6. When cake starts to bubble on top, flip with a spatula and cook on the other side until golden brown.

Serve immediately with butter, sour cream, or salsa.

Garlic Bread

Every now and then, I'll get a wild hair that I'm going on a low-carb diet. It works out well for a few days. But the one food that really makes my mouth water and makes me want to jump off the wagon is toast. If you've never cooked bread in a skillet, you're missing out on one of the Seven Pleasures of the World. Just the smell of the bread cooking in the skillet will make you want to give up everything you own for one bite of it's warm, buttery perfection.

1 Tbsp. butter, softened

¼ tsp. garlic powder

¼ tsp. dried parsley

1 small loaf of bread such as sourdough, Italian, or French bread (choose bread that will fit into your skillet)

1. In small bowl, mix together butter, garlic powder, and dried parsley. Set aside.

2. Slice loaf of bread in half to form an open-face loaf. Cut loaf to fit in your skillet if necessary. If you can't fit both pieces of bread in your skillet, repeat process with second piece.

3. Heat dry skillet over medium heat.

4. Spread butter mixture over open face of bread and place facedown in heated skillet.

5. Using a spatula, check the progress of the bread. This process will only take 1–2 minutes. When bread has reached your desired toastiness, flip it over and allow to heat up on opposite side, 1–2 minutes.

Serve warm as a side dish to a spaghetti dinner.

Cheesy Garlic Bread

This bread is for all of you cheese lovers out there. Choose your favorite cheese blends to use in this recipe.

1 Tbsp. butter, softened

¼ tsp. garlic powder

¼ cup parmesan cheese

¼ cup mozzarella cheese

1 small loaf of bread such as sourdough, Italian, or French bread (choose bread that will fit into your skillet)

1. In a small bowl, mix together butter and garlic powder. Set aside.

2. Slice loaf of bread in half to form an open-face loaf. Cut loaf to fit in your skillet if necessary. If you can't fit both pieces of bread in your skillet, repeat process with the second piece.

3. Heat dry skillet over medium-low heat.

4. Spread butter mixture over open face of bread and place facedown in heated skillet.

5. Using a spatula, check the progress of bread. This process will only take 1–2 minutes. When bread has reached desired toastiness, turn over and lower heat to low. Sprinkle cheese evenly over two pieces of bread. Cover skillet and allow the cheese to melt over the bread, 2–3 minutes.

Serve warm as a side dish to a spaghetti dinner.

Main Dishes

The Power of Necessity

My mother and her mother have the same hands. I have often wondered if I would ever be the kind of woman that my mother is or that her mother was when she was still able. Would I be able to fix things, to create something from nothing? Would I be the woman that my family turns to when they want to make sure that everything would be all right? It is not for me to answer that question. I can only do my best and, in the end, hope that my sons remember me as a woman who did what was necessary.

Putting food on the table for your family is a necessity. The food doesn't have to be fancy or expensive, but it should taste good. Cooking may not come instinctively to you, but it is a skill that can be learned. I learned to cook because my mama took a job working shift work during my senior year of high school. I learned to cook a few simple dishes because it was necessary to feed myself, my brother, and my daddy while she was away. Yes, we did takeout sometimes and my daddy cooked sometimes, but I needed to learn to cook to feel like I was contributing to the family's welfare. Yes, I drained the grease from ground beef down the kitchen sink the first time I attempted to make spaghetti. But I learned from that mistake and didn't make it again.

Sometimes God sends you blessings that feel like hardships. He has blessed me with financial struggles and, from those struggles, I have learned to make something from nothing. I have learned to take a few ingredients, stretch them with rice or pasta, season them well, and create dishes that could be served to kings. I may not have the hands of my mother and her mother, but I share their hearts; hearts that understand the power of necessity.

Chicken Fajita Meatballs

This recipe flittered around in my mind for quite a while before it actually became a reality. I love chicken fajitas and wanted to redistribute the ingredients in a new way. I gauge the success of a recipe by my husband's response to them. He thought these came from a restaurant, so I knew I was on to something good.

2 Tbsp. olive oil

2 bell peppers, thinly sliced

1 large onion, thinly sliced

¼ tsp. salt

½ tsp. fajita seasoning

1 lb. ground chicken

½ cup plain bread crumbs

1 Tbsp. fajita seasoning

1 tsp. salt

¼ cup fresh cilantro, chopped

½ cup chicken broth

Optional garnish: chopped cilantro

1. In a large skillet, heat olive oil over medium-high heat.

2. Add bell peppers and cook for 6–8 minutes.

3. Add onions, salt, and ½ tsp. fajita seasoning. Sauté vegetables until caramelized around the edges, approximately 5 additional minutes. Remove from skillet and set aside.

4. In a mixing bowl, add ground chicken, bread crumbs, tablespoon of fajita seasoning, salt, and cilantro. Mix together and form 1-inch meatballs. If mixture seems sticky, refrigerate for about 10 minutes.

5. Heat the same skillet over medium heat. Add additional olive oil if necessary.

6. Add meatballs and brown on all sides, turning frequently and carefully.

7. Add the chicken broth and reduce heat to medium-low. Cook until chicken broth has been reduced and meatballs are cooked through, approximately 8 minutes.

8. Return the peppers to the skillet and fold gently around the meatballs.

Serve immediately with flour tortillas.

Chicken Potpie Dumplings

Do I want to make chicken potpie or do I want to make chicken and dumplings? Let's combine the two dishes into one. This dish is a labor of love, as are all potpies and chicken and dumplings. But the work will pay off handsomely.

Dumplings:
- 1½ cups flour
- 2 tsp. baking powder
- ¾ tsp. salt
- ½ tsp. pepper
- ¼ tsp. garlic powder
- 3 Tbsp. butter, softened
- ¾ cup milk
- 1 Tbsp. fresh chives, chopped
- 1 Tbsp. fresh parsley, chopped

Chicken mixture:
- 6 cups chicken broth
- 1 onion, chopped
- 3 cloves garlic, finely chopped
- 2 chicken bouillon cubes
- 1 tsp. seasoning salt
- 1 tsp. garlic salt
- ½ tsp. pepper
- 2 large bone-in chicken breasts or equivalent
- ½ cup corn
- ½ cup carrots, finely diced or shredded
- 2 green onions, thinly sliced
- ½ cup heavy whipping cream
- 1 Tbsp. fresh parsley, chopped

Dumplings

1. In mixing bowl, combine flour, baking powder, salt, pepper, and garlic powder. Mix until thoroughly combined.

2. Add butter and milk and stir until mixture comes together. The mixture will be sticky.

3. Fold in chives and parsley.

4. Set aside until ready to use.

Chicken mixture

1. In large, deep skillet, add chicken broth, onions, garlic, bouillon cubes, seasoning salt, garlic salt, and pepper.

2. Bring to boil and add chicken breasts. Lower heat to medium-low and cook chicken until cooked through. Time will vary based on size and type of chicken used.

3. Once chicken is done, remove from broth mixture and allow to cool to the touch. Retain broth mixture.

4. After chicken has cooled enough to handle, remove skin and pull chicken from bones. Return chicken to broth.

5. At this point, taste broth to determine if seasonings are to your taste. Add more seasonings if necessary.

6. Bring mixture back to a boil on medium-high heat.

7. Stir in corn and carrots.

8. After mixture is boiling, use a spoon to drop golf ball-size dumplings into broth. Once all dumplings have been added to mixture, use a spatula to gently separate any dumplings that may be sticking together. Reduce mixture to medium-low heat and allow dumplings to cook through, gently and carefully turning them over halfway through the cooking process. Cook dumplings for approximately 15 minutes.

9. Add the green onions and cream. Cook for another 5 minutes.

10. Turn off the heat and cover the dish. The mixture will thicken upon standing.

11. Sprinkle with parsley before serving.

Chicken, Artichoke & Spinach Pasta

All of the pasta dishes in this cookbook are considered weeknight meals. They can be prepared quickly and don't require a lot of ingredients. They can also be adapted to your taste preferences by substituting different seasonings or adding a sprinkle of cheese.

8 oz. pasta, prepared

3 Tbsp. olive oil, divided

1 large chicken breast, thinly sliced

Sprinkle of garlic salt and pepper

6–8 jarred artichoke quarters, roughly chopped

2 cloves garlic, chopped

6 oz. fresh baby spinach

Sprinkle of salt and pepper

1. Prepare pasta and set aside.

2. In a large skillet, heat one tablespoon of olive oil over medium heat. Add chicken and sprinkle with garlic salt and pepper. Cook until chicken is cooked through, 7–8 minutes. Remove chicken from skillet.

3. Add remaining olive oil.

4. Add artichokes and garlic, cook approximately 1 minute.

5. Add spinach and cook until wilted, 2–3 minutes. Sprinkle with salt and pepper.

6. Return chicken to the mixture.

7. Add pasta and stir all ingredients together.

Serve immediately.

Creamy Chicken Cajun Pasta

Every time I stumble upon this recipe either in my photos or in my cookbook notes, I always have the same reaction: "Man, this is so good!" I hope that you have the same reaction when you cook it for your family. It is as delicious as it is beautiful.

8 oz. pasta, prepared	Pinch of pepper
4 Tbsp. olive oil, divided	2 cloves garlic, finely chopped
1 green bell pepper, thinly sliced	1¼ tsp. Cajun seasoning, divided
1 red bell pepper, thinly sliced	1 lb. chicken, thinly sliced
1 onion, thinly sliced	½ tsp. garlic salt
¼ tsp. salt	½ cup heavy cream

1. Prepare pasta and set aside.

2. In large skillet, add two tablespoons of olive oil and heat over medium heat. Add peppers and cook until softened and caramelized, 6–7 minutes.

3. Add onion. Sprinkle with salt and pepper. Cook for 5 minutes.

4. Add chopped garlic and sprinkle with ¼ teaspoon Cajun seasoning. After garlic is softened, remove pepper mixture from skillet and set aside.

5. Add remaining olive oil to skillet.

6. Add chicken. Sprinkle with garlic salt and remaining Cajun seasoning. Cook until chicken is cooked through, 6–7 minutes.

7. Return pepper mixture to skillet.

8. Add heavy cream. After cream mixture comes to a boil, return pasta to skillet. Stir to coat in sauce.

Serve immediately.

Chicken, Ranch & Bacon Pasta

Calling all ranch dressing lovers! I know you're out there and are looking for yet another way to enjoy your favorite dressing mix. Here you go. This is the perfect meal to throw together after a long day at work and school.

8 oz. pasta, prepared

5 slices bacon, chopped

1 lb. chicken, cubed

1 (1 oz.) pkg. ranch dressing mix

¼ cup chicken broth

¼ cup heavy cream

3 green onions, thinly sliced

1. Prepare pasta and set aside.

2. In large skillet over medium heat, add bacon and cook until crispy. Using a slotted spoon, remove bacon from skillet, reserving one tablespoon of bacon grease in skillet. Set bacon aside.

3. Add chicken to bacon grease and cook until done, approximately 7 minutes.

4. Sprinkle with dressing mix and stir until evenly distributed.

5. Add chicken broth and heavy cream. Cook until bubbly, approximately 5 minutes.

6. Add pasta to mixture and stir until coated.

7. Sprinkle with bacon and green onions.

Serve immediately.

Chicken Fajita Pasta

If you don't want to be bothered with making chicken fajita meatballs, you can get the same flavor profile in this pasta dish. Scoop on some salsa or sour cream at the end to shake things up a bit.

8 oz. pasta, prepared

2 boneless chicken breasts, diced

2 Tbsp. olive oil

2 bell peppers, thinly sliced

1 onion, thinly sliced

2 tsp. fajita seasonings

½ tsp. salt

½ cup heavy cream

2 Tbsp. fresh cilantro, chopped

1. Prepare pasta and set aside.

2. In large skillet, cook chicken in olive oil over medium heat until chicken is browned and cooked through. Remove from heat.

3. Add peppers to remaining oil and cook for approximately 5 minutes.

4. Add onions to peppers and cook for 10 minutes until softened and caramelized around edges.

5. Return chicken to pan.

6. Add fajita seasoning and salt.

7. Add heavy cream and cook until mixture is bubbly and has thickened, approximately 5 minutes.

8. Add pasta to skillet and stir until well coated.

9. Sprinkle with cilantro.

Serve immediately.

Honey Sesame Chicken

I often think that I don't have enough honey in my life. If you feel that you are in the need of a little more honey, try this recipe. If possible, buy honey that is local to your area. Local honey is beneficial to your health and the economy.

¼ cup honey

2 Tbsp. soy sauce

1 tsp. sesame oil

1 tsp. seasoned rice vinegar

3 boneless, skinless chicken breasts

1 tsp. kosher salt

¼ tsp. coarse black pepper

1 Tbsp. cornstarch

2 Tbsp. canola or vegetable oil

1 Tbsp. sesame seeds

Pinch of red pepper flakes (optional)

3 green onions, thinly sliced

1. In a small bowl, combine honey, soy sauce, sesame oil, and rice vinegar and stir until thoroughly blended. Set aside.

2. Cut chicken into bite-size pieces. Put in separate bowl.

3. Sprinkle chicken with salt, pepper, and cornstarch. Stir until chicken is well coated with cornstarch.

4. In a large skillet, heat the oil on medium-high heat. Add chicken and brown on both sides.

5. Lower heat to medium-low and add honey mixture to chicken, stirring to coat chicken. Cook until chicken is cooked through, about 10 minutes.

6. Add sesame seeds and red pepper flakes if desired.

7. Stir again and remove from heat.

8. Add green onions.

Serve immediately over rice.

BBQ Chicken Pasta

If I were to go into my kitchen and count the bottles of barbecue sauce in my cabinet and refrigerator, I would be ashamed to share the total. My husband loves to buy a variety of barbecue sauces and then mix different bottles together along with different spice blends to create a flavor that pleases him. I guess you could call it a hobby of his. Needless to say, I'm always looking for ways to use up barbecue sauce in different dishes. This pasta dish is so good and the flavor could vary widely according to your favorite barbecue sauce.

8 oz. pasta, prepared	¼ cup barbecue sauce
1 Tbsp. olive oil	¼ cup chicken broth
1 lb. chicken breasts, sliced	¼ red onion, finely diced
1 Tbsp. barbecue seasoning	

1. Prepare pasta and set aside.

2. In large skillet, heat olive oil over medium heat.

3. Add chicken and sprinkle with barbecue seasoning. Cook until chicken is cooked through, 7–8 minutes.

4. Add barbecue sauce and chicken broth. Cook until bubbly, 2–3 minutes.

5. Stir in prepared pasta.

6. Sprinkle with onion.

Serve immediately.

Pulled BBQ Chicken

In addition to stockpiling a variety of barbecue sauces, I also like to make my own. This sauce is heavily influenced by South Carolina mustard-style sauce. If you prefer a ketchup-based sauce, reduce the mustard to ¼ cup and increase the ketchup to ½ a cup. My family consumed this chicken quickly—so quickly that I almost think I only dreamed that I made it. Adding thinly sliced red onions and dill pickle chips would make your BBQ sandwich perfect.

½ cup yellow mustard

¼ cup ketchup

2 Tbsp. brown sugar

½ tsp. pepper

3–4 boneless chicken breasts

Salt and pepper

2 Tbsp. olive oil

1. In small bowl, mix together mustard, ketchup, brown sugar, and pepper. Stir until sugar is dissolved. Set aside.

2. Season chicken breasts with desired amount of salt and pepper or preferred seasonings.

3. Heat olive oil in skillet over medium-high heat. Add chicken breasts to skillet, browning both sides. Lower heat and allow chicken to cook through, approximately 10 minutes.

4. When chicken is cooked through, remove from skillet and, using two forks, pull meat into bite-size pieces.

5. Return to skillet and add mustard sauce.

6. Bring to a simmer over medium-low heat. Simmer for 6–7 minutes.

Serve warm on hamburger buns.

Turkey, Ranch & Bacon Meatballs

Instead of using a packet of ranch dressing mix, I brought in the flavors of ranch through the fresh chives and dried seasonings. You could substitute a dressing packet for the ingredients listed here.

4 slices bacon, cooked and finely chopped

1 lb. ground turkey

½ cup plain bread crumbs

2 Tbsp. fresh chives, finely chopped

1 tsp. garlic powder

½ tsp. garlic salt

¼ tsp. pepper

¼ tsp. dried dill

1. In large skillet, fry bacon over medium-high heat until crispy. Remove bacon with a slotted spot, reserving bacon grease in skillet. Finely chop bacon.

2. In a bowl, mix together chopped bacon, ground turkey, bread crumbs, chives, and remaining seasonings until well blended. Shape into 1" meatballs.

3. Heat reserved bacon grease over medium heat. Add meatballs and brown on all sides, turning frequently and carefully. Lower heat and cook meatballs until done, 8–10 minutes.

4. Serve over a bed of sautéed spinach.

Sautéed Spinach with Garlic

1 Tbsp. olive oil

2–3 cloves garlic, chopped

1 (6-oz.) bag fresh baby spinach

Salt and pepper, to taste

1. Heat olive oil in a large skillet over medium-high heat.

2. Add chopped garlic and cook for 1 minute, stirring continuously.

3. Add spinach, lifting oil and garlic from the bottom of the pan to the top of the spinach.

4. Season with salt and pepper. Cook for 2 minutes.

Serve immediately.

Classic Beef Roast with Potatoes & Carrots

Not all of my dishes bring the boys to the yard . . . I mean, the kitchen. However, I've never cooked a roast without an audience of admirers. Choose to make this roast when you have a few hours to devote to the kitchen. Think of the time spent cooking a roast as an investment in your family's happiness.

2 lbs. chuck roast or chuck steaks

½ tsp. seasoning salt

½ tsp. garlic powder

¼ tsp. pepper

2 Tbsp. olive oil

1 onion, finely diced

2 Tbsp. flour

3 cups beef broth

1 Tbsp. dried minced onions

1 cup finely diced or shredded carrots,

4 medium potatoes, finely diced or sliced

1. Season the chuck roast with seasoning salt, garlic powder, and pepper.

2. Heat oil in a large skillet over medium-high heat. Add the roast and brown both sides. Remove the roast from the skillet and set aside.

3. Lower the heat to medium.

4. Add the onions and cook until soft, approximately 5 minutes.

5. Sprinkle in flour. Cook for 1–2 minutes until onions are completely coated with flour.

6. Slowly add in the beef broth and scrape the drippings from the bottom of the pan while stirring in the broth.

7. Sprinkle in the dried minced onions.

8. Return the roast to the skillet. Lower heat to medium-low and cover the skillet. Cook for approximately 2 hours. After the roast has cooked through, carefully remove it from the skillet and shred it with two forks. Return to the skillet. Taste to see if seasonings are correct. Add more seasonings at this point if necessary.

9. Bring the mixture back to a boil over medium-high heat.

10. Add the carrots and potatoes and cook until tender, 10–12 minutes.

Serve with warm, crusty bread.

Salisbury Steak Meatballs with Onion Gravy

Here is food that will soothe the savage beast or a particularly irritated spouse. No matter what has happened during the day, if you can entice your spouse into the kitchen and lift the lid on these beauties, all is forgiven.

1½ lbs. ground beef

1 Tbsp. onion powder

1 Tbsp. Worcestershire sauce

1 tsp. beef bouillon granules or 1 crushed bouillon cube

½ tsp. pepper

½ tsp. seasoning salt

½ cup plain bread crumbs

½ cup vegetable oil

1 onion, finely diced

½ cup flour

1 tsp. seasoning salt

1 tsp. onion powder

¼ tsp. pepper

4 cups beef broth

1. In mixing bowl, combine ground beef, onion powder, Worcestershire sauce, beef bouillon granules, pepper, seasoning salt, and bread crumbs. Form into 1" meatballs. Set aside.

2. In large skillet, heat oil over medium heat. Add meatballs and brown on all sides, turning frequently and carefully, approximately 6 minutes. Remove meatballs from skillet and set aside.

3. Add onion to oil in skillet and sauté until translucent, 3–4 minutes.

4. Add flour, seasoning salt, onion powder, and pepper. Stir until flour has absorbed oil, approximately 2 minutes.

5. Slowly stir in beef broth, scraping bottom of skillet as you go. Bring to boil over medium heat. Carefully taste gravy to check seasonings. Adjust seasonings to taste.

6. Return meatballs to gravy mixture. Lower heat to medium-low and cover skillet.

7. Cook for 15–20 minutes.

Serve immediately over buttered egg noodles.

Chili Macaroni Stew

Often, I will bounce recipe ideas off of my husband just to get an idea if I'm moving in the right direction. When I asked my husband how he felt about a chili recipe that included both ground beef and pieces of roast, he was not receptive to the idea. He was wrong. It's brilliant!

1 lb. ground beef

1 lb. chuck roast or chuck steak, cubed into bite-size pieces

½ tsp. seasoning salt

½ tsp. pepper

½ tsp. garlic powder

2 Tbsp. olive oil

1 (28 oz.) can crushed tomatoes

¼ tsp. baking soda

2 cups chicken broth

1 Tbsp. chili powder

1 tsp. garlic powder

½ tsp. garlic salt

8 oz. short pasta

Optional: shredded cheese, diced onions, sour cream

1. In large skillet, brown ground beef until no longer pink. Remove from skillet, drain fat, and set aside.

2. Sprinkle chuck roast with seasoning salt, pepper, and garlic powder.

3. Heat oil over medium-high heat in skillet. Add roast and brown on all sides.

4. Add ground beef back to skillet.

5. Add crushed tomatoes, baking soda, broth, chili powder, garlic powder, and garlic salt. Bring to boil.

6. Cover and lower heat to medium-low. Cook until roast is tender, approximately 1 hour.

7. Uncover and increase heat to medium-high. Bring to boil.

8. Add pasta and cook until pasta is al dente, then remove from heat.

Serve with shredded cheese, diced onions, or sour cream.

Sloppy Skillet Meat Loaf

There is nothing more comforting than a slice of meat loaf drenched in ketchup sitting on a plate next to creamy mashed potatoes and peppered green beans. To be honest, I don't like making meat loaf. There's just too much to think about: cooking it to the right point of doneness, draining the grease or not draining the grease as it cooks. I don't want to think about it. This recipe deconstructs the traditional meat loaf by serving it in the form of Sloppy Joes but with the traditional flavors of a meat loaf. While I served it over mashed potatoes, you could always serve it on a bun for a sloppy meat loaf sandwich.

Sloppy Skillet Meat Loaf:
1 lb. ground beef
½ tsp. onion powder
½ tsp. pepper
1 tsp. seasoning salt

Sauce:
¾ cup ketchup
2 Tbsp. yellow mustard
1 Tbsp. brown sugar
1 Tbsp. Worcestershire sauce
⅛ tsp. pepper

1. In large skillet, add ground beef, onion powder, pepper, and seasoning salt.

2. Cook over medium heat until cooked through, 7–8 minutes. Drain excess grease and return to skillet.

3. In small bowl, combine sauce ingredients. Stir together until sugar is fully incorporated.

4. Pour sauce mixture over ground beef. Bring to a low simmer and let cook until the sugar is dissolved and the sauce has thickened, approximately 10 minutes.

Serve immediately with mashed potatoes and green beans.

The Story of Spaghetti

There are some foods that, while common in some households, are completely foreign in others. Growing up, that foreign dish was spaghetti. I assume that as a seven-year-old I was familiar with the concept of spaghetti. I had been singing "On top of spaghetti all covered with cheese, I lost my poor meatball, when somebody sneezed" for years. So I knew it existed. However, my mama had never felt the need to make it and introduce me to it.

One evening, around the time of my seventh year, also known as the day my life changed, my family joined my mama's friend's family for dinner in their home. When I was served a plate of spaghetti and took my place kneeling at the family's coffee table, I was overwhelmed with a sense of apprehension and excitement. I had never had spaghetti before. Where was I to begin? Watching the other kids around me, I quickly adapted my eating style and was swirling noodles on my fork within minutes. From that moment on, I was hooked on spaghetti. I still am.

After I told my mama how much I liked the spaghetti, she quickly added it to our menu plan. It was nothing fancy. Pour a jar of spaghetti sauce over cooked ground beef. Cook the spaghetti and serve separate on the side. That's the way we ate it. Noodles always separate so that you could add the amount of sauce that you liked.

At some point, my mema, Mama's mama, learned about spaghetti and decided to try her hand at making it too. But, it was a little different than my mama's spaghetti. I think she used a combination of beef and pork that didn't sit well on my child's palate. Mema had no use for a jarred sauce. She threw in some tomato sauce and salt and pepper. Then she threw the noodles on top of it all, stirring it together. Oh, okay . . . remind me not to visit on spaghetti day.

Years later, after meeting my husband (then boyfriend), we went to visit his parents for the weekend. His mother was an excellent cook and had provided me with some delicious meals. One particular day, she made spaghetti. It was pretty much the exact concoction that Mema had created twenty years before. Interesting. I'm seeing a pattern.

Several years after experiencing my future mother-in-law's spaghetti, I became friends with someone who was significantly younger than me. She was testing the waters in the cooking world by preparing meals for her boyfriend. She told me how she had made a big batch of spaghetti and that her boyfriend didn't like the fact that she had put the noodles in the sauce and stirred them around. He liked the sauce and noodles separate. I said, "Oh my goodness, you make grandma spaghetti."

Grandma's Spaghetti

I have created my own version of what I call Grandma's Spaghetti, with the noodles stirred into the sauce and served in one skillet. The spaghetti expert in my home loved it, so that just proves that there is no right or wrong way to serve spaghetti. Or maybe there is.

16 oz. spaghetti, prepared	2 cups water
1 lb. ground beef	1 tsp. baking soda
1 Tbsp. olive oil	1½ tsp. garlic powder
3–4 garlic cloves, finely diced	1½ tsp. garlic salt
1 (28 oz.) can crushed tomatoes	¼ cup fresh basil, chopped

1. Prepare pasta and set aside. You may also cook pasta in spaghetti sauce after sauce is done.

2. In large skillet, cook ground beef over medium heat until browned and no longer pink. Drain and set aside.

3. To same skillet, add olive oil and garlic. Cook over medium heat for approximately 2 minutes.

4. Add crushed tomatoes and water.

5. Sprinkle in baking soda, garlic powder, and garlic salt.

6. Return ground beef to skillet and stir together. Reduce heat to medium low, cover, and cook for approximately 30 minutes.

7. When sauce is done, add prepared spaghetti and sprinkle in fresh basil. If cooking pasta in sauce, increase the heat to a boil, add pasta, and cook per al dente instructions on package. After pasta is done, sprinkle with basil.

Serve immediately with garlic bread.

Mexican Meatballs

Whenever I make tacos, I've noticed that as the kids eat, the meat falls out of the tortilla. They end up with a taco salad on their plates by the end of the meal. Not that there's anything wrong with that. Who doesn't love a nice taco salad? So I got the idea of forming the taco meat into meatballs to keep them on the tortilla. It worked out nicely. My older son is a huge fan of a locally owned taco restaurant. He could eat there every day. He gave me the ultimate compliment when he tasted these and said they taste just like his favorite taco joint. Victory!

1 cup finely crushed tortilla chips

1 lb. ground beef

1 Tbsp. taco seasoning

½ tsp. garlic salt

2 Tbsp. olive oil

Soft flour or corn tortillas

Suggested toppings: pico de gallo, salsa, sour cream, mexican cheese blend, cilantro

1. Crush tortilla chips by placing in food processor or by crushing in a zippered storage bag using a rolling pin or a heavy can.

2. In mixing bowl, mix together ground beef, crushed tortilla chips, taco seasoning, and garlic salt. Shape into 1" meatballs.

3. In a large skillet, heat olive oil over medium heat. Add meatballs and brown on all sides, turning frequently and carefully. Lower heat and cook until done, 8–10 minutes.

Serve immediately in your favorite tortilla or use as a topping for a taco salad.

Dirty Rice

As I developed recipes for Southern on a Shoestring, *my husband asked if I would be including my recipe for dirty rice. Well, considering that my dirty rice is a boxed mix, I'm going to say no. But it did get me thinking. Could I make a dirty rice from scratch? I think this one worked out well.*

½ lb. ground beef or pork

½ bell pepper, finely diced

½ onion, finely diced

1 Tbsp. olive oil

1 cup rice

1 tsp. Cajun seasoning

½ tsp. salt

½ tsp. garlic powder

2 cups beef broth

1. In a skillet, cook meat until brown over medium heat. Remove meat from pan to drain excess grease. Set aside until ready to use.

2. In same skillet, add bell pepper, onion, and olive oil. Cook until vegetables are soft.

3. Add rice and seasonings. Stir until well coated.

4. Return meat to skillet.

5. Add beef broth.

6. Increase heat to high and allow mixture to come to a boil. Cover skillet and reduce heat to low. Cook for 15–20 minutes until liquid is absorbed.

7. Fluff with fork before serving.

Serve immediately. Buttered corn is the perfect side dish for dirty rice.

Ground Beef & Orzo

The combination of brown sugar, soy sauce, garlic salt, and pepper gives this dish such a unique flavor. The dish comes together very quickly and is perfect for weeknight dinners.

8 oz. orzo, prepared

1 lb. ground beef

2 Tbsp. brown sugar

2 Tbsp. soy sauce

½ tsp. garlic salt

½ tsp. pepper

2 cups beef broth

4–5 green onions, finely diced

1. Prepare orzo according to package directions. Drain and set aside.

2. Cook ground beef in skillet over medium heat until cooked through and no longer pink. Drain meat and return to skillet.

3. Add brown sugar, soy sauce, garlic salt, and pepper. Stir until meat is coated.

4. Add in beef broth and bring mixture to a boil over medium heat for 6–8 minutes.

5. Stir in prepared orzo.

6. Sprinkle with green onions.

Serve immediately.

Red Rice with Sausage

While I included a whole sausage in this recipe, you could easily get away with only using half of a sausage. Whenever I'm stretching my food budget, I'll only use half a sausage and save the other half for a meal later in the week.

1-14 oz. kielbasa sausage, thinly sliced and diced	1 cup rice
	1 tsp. salt
2 Tbsp. olive oil	¼ tsp. Creole seasoning
1 green bell pepper, thinly sliced	1 (14.5 oz.) can crushed tomatoes
1 onion, thinly sliced	¾ cup water

1. Add sausage and olive oil to skillet. Cook sausage over medium heat until heated through. Remove sausage from skillet, retaining oil, and set aside.

2. Add bell pepper to skillet and cook for 6–7 minutes.

3. Add onions to peppers and cook for an additional 5 minutes.

4. Add rice, salt, and Creole seasoning to vegetable mixture. Stir to evenly coat ingredients in oil and seasonings.

5. Add crushed tomatoes and water.

6. Return sausage to skillet.

7. Increase heat to medium-high and bring mixture to a boil. Cover skillet and lower heat to low. Cook until liquid has been absorbed, 20–25 minutes.

Stir rice to evenly distribute sausage and vegetables before serving.

Italian Sausage with Peppers & Onions

As I slowly creep toward middle age (some would say I'm already there), I find that I am broadening my taste horizons. I used to hate Italian sausage, but I've learned to embrace the flavor and have started using it quite often. I buy one-pound packages of bulk sausage at my local grocery store. I often cut the package in half to use in two different recipes. Feel free to use a whole pound of sausage if you choose.

---

8 oz. pasta, prepared

2 bell peppers, thinly sliced

2 Tbsp. olive oil

1 onion, thinly sliced

2 cloves garlic, finely chopped

¼ tsp. salt and pepper

½ tsp. garlic salt

½ lb. Italian sausage

Optional: pinch of red pepper flakes

---

1. Prepare pasta and set aside.

2. In a large skillet, add bell peppers and olive oil. Cook on medium heat for approximately 6 minutes.

3. Add onion, chopped garlic, salt, pepper, and garlic salt to peppers and cook for additional 6 minutes.

4. Remove mixture from skillet and set aside.

5. Add sausage to skillet and cook until brown.

6. Return pepper mixture to skillet and stir mixture together.

7. Add prepared pasta to skillet and toss to blend ingredients. Drizzle in more olive oil and sprinkle in red pepper flakes if desired.

Serve immediately.

Sausage, Spinach & Garlic Pasta

This is another dish that is perfect when you don't have a lot of time to spend in the kitchen. Substitute sausage with ground beef, turkey, or chicken if desired.

8 oz. short pasta, prepared

½ lb. sausage, browned

4–5 cloves garlic, finely chopped

6 oz. fresh baby spinach

¼ tsp. pepper

⅛ tsp. salt

1. Prepare pasta and set aside.

2. In a skillet, cook sausage over medium heat, adding garlic halfway through cooking. Cook until sausage is cooked through, 8–10 minutes.

3. Add spinach to the sausage mixture.

4. Sprinkle with pepper and salt.

5. Stir in the pasta until fully incorporated.

Serve immediately.

Fried Cabbage with Sausage & Ginger

After you eat fried cabbage, you'll never go back to eating boiled cabbage. The first time my husband made this dish for me, he sprinkled in some grated ginger. It just adds a little spicy burst that is delicious. This dish would be just as delicious without the sausage. Just add a little extra seasoning.

1-14 oz. kielbasa sausage	1 Tbsp. freshly grated ginger
1 whole cabbage	Salt and pepper to taste
1 Tbsp. olive oil	

1. Slice sausage into bite-size pieces. Set aside.

2. Cut cabbage into quarters and remove the core. Next, cut into bite-size pieces and set aside.

3. In large skillet, add sliced sausage and olive oil. Cook over medium heat until sausage starts to brown. Remove from skillet and set aside.

4. Add cabbage and continue cooking over medium heat for approximately 5 minutes before adding ginger. Continue cooking for an additional 5–10 minutes until cabbage has softened and edges are golden brown.

5. Return sausage to skillet.

6. Sprinkle with desired amount of salt and pepper.

Serve immediately.

Spring Green Shrimp Pasta

I used to be a purist when it came to asparagus. I would only eat it roasted because I couldn't bear the thought of cutting it into bite-size pieces and throwing it in a dish. But I decided to set aside my prejudices and try something new. Now I like to put asparagus in as many dishes as I can. Asparagus is always cheaper in the spring, but this dish can be made any time of the year.

8 oz. prepared pasta

1 lb. fresh asparagus

1 Tbsp. olive oil

Pinch of salt and pepper

10 oz. shrimp, peeled and deveined

¼ tsp. salt

¼ tsp. pepper

½ tsp. garlic powder

2 Tbsp. olive oil

4–5 green onions, thinly sliced

Optional: ¼ cup fresh parsley, finely chopped

1. Prepare pasta and set aside.

2. Cut off and discard woody ends of the asparagus. Cut remaining stalks into 1" pieces.

3. In a large skillet, heat 1 tablespoon of olive oil over medium heat. Add asparagus and salt and pepper. Cook until asparagus is slightly tender but still bright green, approximately 8–9 minutes. Remove from heat and set aside.

4. Sprinkle shrimp with salt, pepper, and garlic powder.

5. Add additional olive oil to skillet and heat on medium heat.

6. Add shrimp to skillet and cook for approximately 5 minutes until done.

7. Return asparagus to skillet and add green onions. Toss together.

8. Add prepared pasta and toss until coated with olive oil. Additional olive oil may be used if desired.

9. Sprinkle in parsley if desired.

Serve immediately.

Buffalo Shrimp Pasta

Oh my goodness! I have made this dish so many times since creating it for this book. It's probably my favorite recipe here. I love everything about it, especially how few ingredients it has, how quickly it comes together, and, most importantly, how it tastes. The flavor is perfection. Add as little or as much hot sauce as you can stand.

8 oz. pasta, prepared

1 lb. medium shrimp, peeled and deveined

½ tsp. garlic powder

Pinch each of salt and pepper

2 Tbsp. olive oil

2 Tbsp. butter

1 Tbsp. hot sauce

2 Tbsp. fresh chives, finely chopped

1. Prepare pasta and set aside.

2. Sprinkle shrimp with garlic powder, salt, and pepper. Heat oil in skillet over medium heat. Add seasoned shrimp. Cook until done, approximately 5–6 minutes depending on size.

3. Add butter and hot sauce and stir until butter is melted.

4. Add prepared pasta to dish and toss ingredients together. Sprinkle with chives.

Serve immediately.

Mexican Shrimp Pasta

Although shrimp is more expensive per pound than other meats, including small amounts of shrimp in dishes like this one allows your family to get a taste of shrimp without breaking the bank. I occasionally find frozen shrimp on sale and I'll pick up a few bags for the freezer. Frozen shrimp thaw fairly quickly or you can rinse them for several minutes in a colander under cold running water.

8 oz. pasta, prepared

10–12 oz. medium shrimp, peeled and deveined

1 tsp. taco seasoning

¼ tsp. salt

1 Tbsp. olive oil

1 Tbsp. butter

4 green onions, thinly sliced

¼ cup fresh cilantro, finely chopped

1. Prepare pasta and set aside.

2. Sprinkle shrimp with taco seasoning and salt. In a large skillet, heat olive oil over medium heat. Add shrimp and cook until done, approximately 5–6 minutes depending on size.

3. Add butter and green onions. Stir until butter is melted.

4. Add in prepared pasta and toss until pasta is coated.

5. Sprinkle in cilantro.

Serve immediately.

Low Country Boil Fried Rice

When my husband cooks Low Country Boil, we often have leftovers for a couple of days. I quickly grow weary of the leftovers and look for other ways to use them. This Low Country Boil fried rice is the perfect way to use up some of the leftovers. To make your life even easier, pick up a small carton of fried rice from your local Chinese restaurant to use in this.

1 Tbsp. olive oil	1 tsp. seafood seasoning
1 cup cooked shrimp	2 Tbsp. olive oil
1 cup corn	4 cups rice, cooked and chilled
1-14 oz. sausage, cooked and diced	4–5 Tbsp. soy sauce
	½ tsp. seafood seasoning

1. In large skillet, heat olive oil over medium heat.

2. Add shrimp, corn, sausage, and seafood seasoning. Cook until heated through, approximately 5 minutes. Remove from skillet and set aside.

3. In same skillet, add additional olive oil and increase heat to medium-high. Add cold rice, soy sauce, and seafood seasoning. Stir until rice is coated with soy sauce and heated through.

4. Return shrimp mixture to rice and stir together.

Serve immediately.

Seared Scallops over Buttery Spinach

Cooking scallops is a rare occurrence in my home due to the fact that they can be fairly expensive. About once a year, I'll break down and splurge on some scallops to make a dish for a special occasion such as a birthday or anniversary. Serve over a bed of spinach with traditional yellow rice.

1 lb. scallops	Juice of half a lemon
¼ tsp. salt	6 oz. fresh baby spinach
½ tsp. seafood seasoning	1 Tbsp. butter
2 Tbsp. olive oil	Pinch of salt and pepper

1. Dry scallops with a paper towel and sprinkle with salt and seafood seasoning.

2. Heat olive oil in a skillet over medium heat.

3. Carefully add scallops to skillet and cook until golden brown before turning to other side, approximately 2 minutes per side depending on size of scallops.

4. Squeeze or sprinkle lemon juice over scallops.

5. Remove scallops from skillet.

6. Add spinach and butter to skillet. Sprinkle with salt and pepper. Cook until spinach wilts, about 1 minute.

Serve scallops immediately on a bed of spinach.

Cooking Measurement Equivalents

Cups	Tablespoons	Fluid Ounces
⅛ cup	2 Tbsp.	1 fl. oz.
¼ cup	4 Tbsp.	2 fl. oz.
⅓ cup	5 Tbsp. + 1 tsp.	
½ cup	8 Tbsp.	4 fl. oz.
⅔ cup	10 Tbsp. + 2 tsp.	
¾ cup	12 Tbsp.	6 fl. oz.
1 cup	16 Tbsp.	8 fl. oz.

Cups	Fluid Ounces	Pints/Quarts/Gallons
1 cup	8 fl. oz.	½ pint
2 cups	16 fl. oz.	1 pint = ½ quart
3 cups	24 fl. oz.	1½ pints
4 cups	32 fl. oz.	2 pints = 1 quart
8 cups	64 fl. oz.	2 quarts = ½ gallon
16 cups	128 fl. oz.	4 quarts = 1 gallon

Other Helpful Equivalents

1 Tbsp.	3 tsp.
8 oz.	½ lb.
16 oz.	1 lb.

Metric Measurement Equivalents

Approximate Weight Equivalents

Ounces	Pounds	Grams
4 oz.	¼ lb.	113 g
5 oz.		142 g
6 oz.		170 g
8 oz.	½ lb.	227 g
9 oz.		255 g
12 oz.	¾ lb.	340 g
16 oz.	1 lb.	454 g

Approximate Volume Equivalents

Cups	US Fluid Ounces	Milliliters
⅛ cup	1 fl. oz.	30 ml
¼ cup	2 fl. oz.	59 ml
½ cup	4 fl. oz.	118 ml
¾ cup	6 fl. oz.	177 ml
1 cup	8 fl. oz.	237 ml

Other Helpful Equivalents

½ tsp.	2½ ml
1 tsp.	5 ml
1 Tbsp.	15 ml

Notes

Index

About the Author

With a bachelor's degree in English, **Kim McCallie** began writing the food blog *A Well-Seasoned Life* in 2010. In addition to the blog, she wrote a weekly food column for her local newspaper, *Effingham Now*, a branch of the Savannah News Press. She is the author of *Southern on a Shoestring*, also published by Cedar Fort. Kim lives near Savannah, Georgia, with her husband, Eric, and their two sons.

SCAN to visit

www.wellseasonedlife.net